JOKES for KIDS

ACTUALLY.
LITERALLY.
SRSLY. BEST.
JOKES. EVER.

CHANTELLE GRACE

BroadStreet
KIDS

BroadStreet Kids
Savage, Minnesota, USA

BroadStreet Kids is an imprint of BroadStreet Publishing Group, LLC.
Broadstreetpublishing.com

JOKES FOR KIDS-BUNDLE ONE

9781424566532
Content compiled by Chantelle Grace.

Typesetting and design by Garborg Design Works | garborgdesign.com
Editorial services by Michelle Winger | literallyprecise.com

Printed in China.

23 24 25 26 27   7 6 5 4 3 2 1

Author Bio

CHANTELLE GRACE is a witty wordsmith who loves music, art, and competitive games. She is fascinated by God's intricate design of the human body, and, as a nurse, she knows it's important to share the gift of laughter with those around her.

TABLE OF CONTENTS....

BEST JOKES EVER

ACTUALLY BEST JOKES EVER

LITERALLY BEST JOKES EVER

SRSLY BEST JOKES EVER

BEST. JOKES. EVER.

JOKES for KIDS

CHANTELLE GRACE

EDUCATION ENTERTAINMENT

Why was the math book sad?

Because it had too many problems.

Why were the teacher's eyes crossed?

She couldn't control her pupils.

Why did the boy eat his homework?

Because his teacher told him it was a piece of cake.

Which weighs more, a ton of feathers
or a ton of bricks?

Neither, they both weigh a ton.

What did the janitor say when he
jumped out of the closet?

"Supplies!"

Why was the student's
report card wet?

It was below C level.

What did one pencil say
to the other pencil?

"You're looking sharp."

Where do pencils go on vacation?

Pennsylvania.

Why did the girl bring lipstick and eye shadow to school?

She had a make-up test.

Why should you take a pencil to bed?

To draw the curtains.

How many books can you put in an empty backpack?

One. After that, it's not empty.

How many letters are in The Alphabet?

There are 11 letters in "The Alphabet."

The turtle took two chocolates to Texas to teach Thomas to tie his boots. How many t's are in that?

There are two t's in that.

GEOGRAPHY GIGGLES

Teacher: Where is the English Channel?

Student: I don't know. My TV doesn't pick it up.

What is the capital of Alaska?

Come on, Juneau this one.

What rock group has four men that don't sing?

Mount Rushmore.

What city cheats at exams?

Peking.

What is the capital of Washington?

The W.

What did Delaware?

Her New Jersey.

What is the fastest country
in the world?

Rush-a.

Teacher: What can you tell me
about the Dead Sea?

*Student: I didn't even know
it was sick.*

What are the Great Plains?

The 747, Concorde, and F-16.

What has five eyes and is lying
on the water?

The Mississippi River.

What did one US flag say to the other?

Nothing, it just waved.

What do you find in the middle
of nowhere?

The letter "h."

What do you call a nutty dog
in Australia?

A dingo-ling.

What birds are found in Portugal?

Portu-geese.

How do you repair a car in Scotland?

With scotch tape.

PIRATE PLAY

Why are pirates called pirates?

Cause they arrrrr.

Why does it take pirates so long
to learn the alphabet?

Because they spend years at C.

How much did the pirate pay
for his earrings?

A buccaneer.

What is a pirate's favorite subject?

Arrrrrrt.

How much did the pirate pay for his hook and peg leg?

An arm and a leg.

Why can't you take a picture of a pirate with a wooden leg?

Because a wooden leg doesn't take pictures.

What do you call a pirate with two eyes and two legs?

A rookie.

What is a pirate's favorite country?

Arrrrrrgentina.

What grades did the pirate get in school?

High C's.

Why didn't the pirate's phone work?

Because he left it off the hook.

What are pirates afraid of?

The darrrrrk.

What do you call a pirate that skips class?

Captain Hooky.

Why didn't the pirate go to the movies?

Because it was arrrrrr rated.

What has eight legs and eight eyes?

Eight pirates.

MUSICAL MADNESS

How do you make a band stand?

Take their chairs away.

What do little penguins sing when their father brings fish home for dinner?

Freeze a Jolly Good Fellow.

What do you get if you cross a sweet potato and a jazz musician?

A yam session.

Why is a piano so hard to open?

Because the keys are on the inside.

What's the most musical bone?

The trom-bone.

Why was the musician arrested?

Because she got in treble.

Why is slippery ice like music?

If you don't C sharp; you'll B flat.

What was the result when a piano fell down a mine shaft?

A-flat minor.

What was stolen from the music store?

The lute.

How do you make a tissue dance?

Put a little boogey in it.

What do you get when you cross
a fridge with a radio?

Cool music.

Why did Mozart get rid of his chickens?

They kept saying Bach, Bach.

Why couldn't the athlete listen
to her music?

Because she broke the record.

What type of music are balloons
afraid of?

Pop music.

FOOD FUNNIES

When do you go at red and stop at green?

> *When you're eating a watermelon.*

Why did the man lose his job at the orange juice factory?

> *He couldn't concentrate.*

What do you repair a tomato with?

> *Tomato Paste.*

What did the hamburger name his daughter?

> *Patty.*

What did the grape do when it got stepped on?

It let out a little wine.

Why do sharks live in salt water?

Because pepper makes them sneeze.

What did Bacon say to Tomato?

"Lettuce get together."

What is a bubbles least favorite drink?

Soda POP.

What did one plate say to the other?

"Dinner's on me."

What is black, white, green, and bumpy?

A pickle wearing a tuxedo.

What's the best thing to put into a pie?

Your teeth.

Patron: Waiter, this food tastes
kind of funny.

Waiter: Then why aren't you laughing?

Why do the French like to eat snails?

Because they don't like fast food.

Why shouldn't you tell an egg a joke?

Because it might crack up.

What did the baby corn say
to its mom?

"Where is pop corn?"

What do you call candy that is stolen?

Hot chocolate.

What kind of nuts always seems
to have a cold?

Cashews.

Waiter, will my pizza be long?

"No sir, it will be round."

What is green and sings?

Elvis Parsley.

Why did the banana go to the doctor?

Because it wasn't peeling well.

What candy do you eat
on the playground?

Recess pieces.

What do dwarves
make sandwiches with?

Shortbread.

Why shouldn't you tell a secret
on a farm?

Because corn has ears.

What is a pretzel's favorite dance?

The Twist.

What are twins' favorite fruit?

Pears.

If a crocodile makes shoes,
what does a banana make?

Slippers.

What do you give to a sick lemon?

Lemon aid.

ANIMAL ANTICS

What happened to the dog that swallowed a firefly?

It barked with de-light.

What kind of key opens a banana?

A monkey.

Why do gorillas have big nostrils?

Because they have big fingers.

Who's the penguin's favorite Aunt?

Aunt-Arctica.

What is a shark's favorite sci-fi show?

Shark Trek.

How does a lion greet the other animals in the field?

"Pleased to eat you."

How do you know that carrots are good for your eyesight?

Rabbits never wear glasses.

Why don't dogs make good dancers?

Because they have two left feet.

Why did the monkey like the banana?

Because it had appeal.

When is a dog not a dog?

When it is pure bred.

What's white, furry, and shaped like a tooth?

A molar bear.

How do bears keep their den cool in summer?

They use bear conditioning.

Why don't you have to tell an elephant a secret more than once?

Because elephants never forget.

What's a penguin's favorite salad?

Iceberg lettuce.

What do you call a solitary shark?

A lone shark.

What dog keeps the best time?

A watch dog.

Why didn't the boy believe the tiger?

He thought it was a lion.

What do you get
from a pampered cow?

Spoiled milk.

What do you get when you cross fish
and an elephant?

Swimming trunks.

Why is a fish easy to weigh?

Because it has its own scales.

Why was the rabbit so upset?

She was having a bad hare day.

What did the banana say
to the monkey?

Nothing, bananas can't talk.

What happens when a frog parks
in a no-parking space?

It gets toad away.

What does a twenty-pound mouse say
to a cat?

"Here kitty, kitty, kitty."

What is a frog's favorite exercise?

Jumping Jacks.

What type of horses only go out
at night?

Nightmares.

What do you call a bear with no teeth?

A gummy bear.

What snakes are found on cars?

Windshield vipers.

What do you get when a chicken lays an egg on top of a barn?

An eggroll.

Why are frogs so happy?

They eat whatever bugs them.

What did the pony say when it had a sore throat?

"I'm a little hoarse."

Why are elephants so wrinkled?

They take too long to iron.

When is a well-dressed lion like a weed?

When he's a dandelion.

What has 12 legs, six eyes, three tails, and can't see?

Three blind mice.

What do monkeys do for laughs?

They tell jokes about people.

What do you call a bear with no ears?

B.

What is an owl's favorite subject?

Owl-gebra.

Why did the snake cross the road?

To get to the other ssssssside.

What is a cat's favorite color?

Purr-ple.

What fish only swims at night?

A starfish.

How do you get down off an elephant?

You don't, you get down off a duck.

Why did the penguin cross the road?

To go with the floe.

What sport don't you want to play
with an elephant?

Squash.

What happened to the lost cattle?

Nobody's herd.

What's gray, squeaky, and hangs around
in caves?

Stalagmice.

Why did the elephant color himself
different colors?

So he could hide in the crayon box.

What do you call an owl
with a deep voice?

A growl.

Where do penguins go to the movies?

At the dive-in.

What do you get when you cross
a snake and a pie?

A pie-thon.

How does a penguin make pancakes?

With its flippers.

Why can't you shock cows?

They've herd it all.

Why are there some fish at the bottom
of the ocean?

Because they dropped out of school.

How many tickles does it take to make
an octopus laugh?

Ten-tickles.

How do bees get to school?

By school buzz.

Where do polar bears vote?

The North Poll.

What do you get if you cross a stuffed bear with a pig?

A teddy boar.

Why are snakes hard to fool?

You can't pull their leg.

Why didn't the chicken cross the road?

Because there was a KFC on the other side.

Why did the owl say, "Tweet, tweet"?

Because she didn't give a hoot.

What animal has more lives than a cat?

Frogs—they croak every night.

Why did the chicken cross the road?

To show everyone he wasn't chicken.

How do you raise a baby elephant?

With a fork lift.

What do you call a dancing sheep?

A baa-lerina.

Where do hamsters come from?

Hamsterdam.

Someone said you sounded like an owl.

"Who?"

What is gray and blue and very big?

An elephant holding its breath.

Where do penguins go to dance?

The snow ball.

What do you give a sick horse?

Cough stirrup.

What is a baby owl after
it is six days old?

Seven days old.

What do penguins have for lunch?

Icebergers.

Two flies are on the porch.
Which one is an actor?

The one on the screen.

What is the biggest ant in the world?

An elephant.

Why was the baby ant confused?

Because all of his uncles were ants.

Why do bees have sticky hair?

Because they have honeycombs.

What animals are the best pets?

Cats, because they are purr-fect.

What do you call a great dog detective?

Sherlock Bones.

What do you call a sheep that is always quiet?

A shhhheep.

What do you call young dogs who play in the snow?

Slush puppies.

What do you call a crate of ducks?

A box of quackers.

What type of markets do dogs avoid?

Flea markets.

Why did the birdie go
to the candy store?

It wanted a tweet.

Why do male deer need braces?

Because they have buck teeth.

What's yellow, weighs 1,000 pounds,
and sings?

Two 500-pound canaries.

What do you get when you cross
a sheep and a honey bee?

Bah-humbug.

SPACE SLAPSTICK

What did Mars say to Saturn?

"Give me a ring sometime."

When is the moon the heaviest?

When it's full.

When do astronauts eat?

At launch time.

What type of songs
do the planets sing?

Nep-tunes.

What is an astronaut's favorite key
on a keyboard?

The space bar.

How do you get a baby astronaut
to sleep?

You rocket.

What's the astronaut's favorite candy
bar?

A Mars bar.

Why did the sun want to go to college?

To brighten its future.

Where did the astronaut park
her spaceship?

A parking meteor.

What was the first animal in space?

The cow that jumped over the moon.

What did the alien say to the cat?

"Take me to your litter."

Why did the astronaut retire?

He got spaced out.

How do astronauts eat
their ice cream?

In floats.

How does one astronaut on the moon
tell another astronaut that he is sorry?

He Apollogises.

NUTTY NATURE

Where does a tree store their stuff?

In their trunk.

What kind of shorts do clouds wear?

Thunderwear.

Why did the tree go to the dentist?

It needed a root canal.

What falls but never hits the ground?

The temperature.

What do you call an attractive volcano?

Lavable.

What did the tree wear
to the pool party?

Swimming trunks.

What did the cloud say
to the lightning bolt?

"You're shocking."

What did the beaver say to the tree?

"It's been nice gnawing you."

Why did the leaf go to the doctor?

It was feeling green.

What is a tree's least favorite month?

Septimber.

What did the tornado say to the sports car?

"Want to go for a spin?"

What kind of tree can fit into your hand?

A palm tree.

How do trees get on the internet?

They log in.

What's a tornado's favorite game?

Twister.

How do hurricanes see?

With one eye.

SPORTS SILLIES

What is a cheerleader's favorite food?

Cheerios.

Why is basketball such a messy sport?

Because everyone dribbles on the floor.

You can serve it, but you can't eat it. What is it?

A volleyball.

Why did the soccer player bring string to the game?

He wanted to tie the score.

Why is a baseball team similar
to a muffin?

They both depend on the batter.

Why do golfers wear two pairs of pants?

In case they get a hole in one.

Why did the man run around his bed?

*Because he wanted to catch up
on his sleep.*

What do you call a boomerang
that doesn't work?

A stick.

Why did the football coach go
to the bank?

He wanted his quarter back.

What is harder to catch the faster you run?

Your breath.

Why is tennis such a loud sport?

The players raise a racquet.

Why did Tarzan spend so much time on the golf course?

He was perfecting his swing.

Why did the ballerina quit?

Because it was tutu hard.

TRANSPORTATION THRILLS

What has four wheels and flies?

A garbage truck.

Which driver never gets a parking ticket?

A screw-driver.

What happened to the wooden car with a wooden engine?

It wooden go.

Which part of a car is always tired?

The exhaust pipe.

What is a car's favorite type of shoes?

Vans.

What do you call a person who draws animations on vehicles?

A car-toonist.

What song does the car like to play?

A car-tune.

What did the jack say to the car?

"Can I give you a lift?"

Why is an old car similar to a baby toy?

They both rattle.

What part of the car is the laziest?

The wheels, because they are always tired.

When do cars get the most flat tires?

When there's a fork in the road.

What car can drive over the water?

Any car that goes across a bridge.

HOME HYSTERIA

Did you hear the joke about the roof?

Never mind, it's over your head.

What can go up a chimney down,
but can't go down a chimney up?

An umbrella.

What did one toilet say to the other?

"You look a bit flushed."

What did one wall say to the other wall?

"I'll meet you at the corner."

Why did the boy throw the clock
out the window?

> *He wanted to see time fly.*

When is a door not a door?

> *When it is ajar.*

Why do fluorescent lights hum?

> *Because they forgot the words.*

Why did the house go to the doctor?

> *Because it had a window pane.*

What gives you the power
to walk through walls?

> *A door.*

What gets wetter the more it dries?

> *A towel.*

How do you warm up a room after it's been painted?

Give it a second coat.

Why was the broom late?

It over swept.

What has one head, one foot, and four legs?

A bed.

What did the blanket say to the bed?

"Don't worry, I've got you covered."

HISTORY HILARITY

What happened when the wheel
was invented?

It caused a revolution.

Why were the early days of history
called the dark ages?

Because there were so many knights.

How were the first Americans like ants?

They also lived in colonies.

What does the Statue of Liberty
stand for?

It can't sit down.

Where did the pilgrims land when they came to America?

On their feet.

How did the Vikings send secret messages?

By norse code.

Who invented fractions?

Henry the 1/4th.

What did they do at the Boston Tea Party?

I don't know, I wasn't invited.

What did Mason say to Dixon?

"We've got to draw the line here."

Who made King Arthur's round table?

Sir-Cumference.

What do Alexander the Great and Kermit the Frog have in common?

The same middle name.

Where was the Declaration of Independence signed?

At the bottom.

Why did the pioneers cross the country in covered wagons?

Because they didn't want to wait forty years for a train.

How was the Roman Empire cut in half?

With a pair of Caesars.

FAIRYTALE FUN

How do you find a princess?

You follow the foot prince.

Why do dragons sleep during the day?

So they can fight knights.

What did the damsel in distress say when her photos did not show up?

"Someday my prints will come."

What kind of car does Mickey Mouse's wife drive?

A Minnie van.

What do you call a rabbit with fleas?

Bugs Bunny.

What did Winnie the Pooh say
to his agent?

"Show me the honey!"

Why did Mickey Mouse take a trip
into space?

He wanted to find Pluto.

Why can't you give Elsa a balloon?

Because she'll let it go.

Why are there no planes where Peter
Pan lives?

*Because there is a sign that says
"Never Neverland."*

What did Nala say to Simba during
the stampede?

"Move fasta."

Why does Alice ask so many questions?
Because she is in Wonder land.

What does Pooh Bear call his girlfriend?
Hunny.

What is Peter Pan's favorite restaurant?
Wendy's.

Where can you find a little mermaid?
Under the sea.

Who is Wall-E's cousin?
Floor-E.

What does Ariel like on her toast?
Mermalade.

What did Woody say to Buzz Lightyear?
A lot. There were three movies.

Why was Cinderella so bad at soccer?

Because she was always running away from the ball, she kept losing her shoes, and she had a pumpkin for a coach.

Why did Arlo help Spot cross the road?

Because he was "The Good Dinosaur."

Why did Sleepy take firewood to bed with him?

He wanted to sleep like a log.

Why did Sven try to eat Olaf's nose?

Because he doesn't carrot all.

What is Mickey Mouse's favorite sport?

Minnie-golf.

What do you call a fairy who doesn't bathe for a year?

Stinker Bell.

What do Bongo and Lulubelle need to live?

Just the bear necessities.

What is Grumpy's favorite fruit?

Sour Grapes.

What kind of blush does Mulan wear?

Mulan Rouge.

What do you get when you cross Winnie-the-Pooh and a skunk?

Winnie the P.U.

Why does Snow White always treat each of the Seven Dwarfs equally?

Because she's the fairest of them all.

Where did Captain Hook get his hook?

From the second hand store.

MEDIA MERRIMENT

What do you say when you lose
a wii game?

"I want a wii-match."

What never asks questions but receives
a lot of answers?

The phone.

What kind of dance did the computer
go to?

A disc-o dance.

What's the difference between a TV and a newspaper?

Ever tried swatting a fly with a TV?

What did the spider do on the computer?

Made a website.

What did the computer do at lunchtime?

Had a byte.

What does a baby computer call his father?

Data.

Why did the computer keep sneezing?

It had a virus.

What is a computer virus?

A terminal illness.

Why was the computer cold?

It left its Windows open.

Why was there a bug in the computer?

Because it was looking for a byte to eat.

Why did the computer squeak?

Because someone stepped on its mouse.

What do you get when you cross a computer and a life guard?

A screensaver.

Where do all the cool mice live?

In their mousepads.

WEATHER WIT

What goes up when the rain comes down?

An umbrella.

Why do Eskimos do their laundry in Tide?

Because it's too cold out-tide.

What season is it when you bounce on a trampoline?

Spring.

Why do birds fly south for the winter?

It's quicker than walking.

What goes up and down
but doesn't move?

The temperature.

Why is England the wettest country?

*Because the queen has reigned there
for years.*

What did one volcano say to the other?

"I lava you."

What bow can't be tied?

A rainbow.

What happens when the fog disappears
in California?

UCLA.

How hot is it?

*It's so hot, when I turned on the
sprinkler, all I got was steam!*

Who does everyone listen to,
but no one believes?

The weatherman.

What is the opposite of a cold front?

A warm back.

Why was there thunder and lightning
in the lab?

The scientists were brainstorming.

What do you do when it's raining cats
and dogs?

Watch out for the poodles.

DINOSAUR DRAMA

What does a triceratops sit on?

Its tricera-bottom.

What do you call a sleeping dinosaur?

A dino-snore.

Why did the Archaeopteryx catch
the worm?

Because it was an early bird.

What was T. Rex's favorite number?

Ate.

Why did the dinosaur get in bed?

Because he was tired.

What do you call a fossil that doesn't ever want to work?

Lazy bones.

What did the dinosaur say after the car crash?

I'm-so-saurus.

What do you call it when a dinosaur makes a goal?

A dino-score.

What do you call a dinosaur with no eyes?

Do-ya-think-he-saw-us.

What's the best way to talk to a Tyrannosaur?

Long distance.

What do you say when you meet
a two-headed dinosaur?

"Hello, hello."

Is it true that a dinosaur won't attack
if you hold a tree branch?

It depends on how fast you carry it.

What makes more noise
than a dinosaur?

Two dinosaurs.

What do you call a Stegosaurus
with carrots in its ears?

Anything you want; it can't hear you.

What do you call a dinosaur that never
gives up?

Try-Try-Try-ceratops.

What's better than a talking dinosaur?

A spelling bee.

What kind of dinosaur can you ride
in a rodeo?

A bronco-saurus.

What do you get when you cross
a dinosaur with fireworks?

Dino-mite.

When can three giant dinosaurs get
under one umbrella and not get wet?

When it's not raining.

Which type of dinosaur could jump
higher than a house?

Any kind. A house can't jump.

What do you do if you find a blue Ichthyosaur?

Cheer him up.

Why don't dinosaurs ever forget?

Because no one ever tells them anything.

Do you know how long dinosaurs should be fed?

Exactly the same as short dinosaurs.

What do you need to know to teach a dinosaur tricks?

More than the dinosaur.

Where was the dinosaur when the sun went down?

In the dark.

What happened when the dinosaur took the train home?

She had to bring it back.

How do you know if there's a dinosaur under your bed?

Your nose hits the ceiling.

Why was the dinosaur afraid of the ocean?

Because there was something fishy about it.

What do you call a dinosaur that left its armor out in the rain?

A stegosaurust.

How do you know if there's a dinosaur in your refrigerator?

Look for footprints in the pizza.

HOLIDAY HUMOR

What is a cow's favorite day?

Moo-years day.

What did the light bulb say to her man on Valentine's Day?

"I love you watts and watts."

Where does the Easter bunny get his breakfast?

IHOP.

How does the Easter bunny stay in shape?

Lots of eggsercise.

What was the most popular dance
in 1776?

Indepen-dance.

What do you call a fake stone
in Ireland?

A sham rock.

Why is St. Patrick's Day most frogs'
favorite holiday?

*Because they are already
wearing green.*

What's a four-leaf clover's favorite
dance?

The shamrock shake.

What is the fear of Santa Claus called?

Claustrophobia.

What nationality is Santa Claus?

North Polish.

What does Tarzan sing at Christmas?

Jungle Bells.

Why does Santa have a garden?

So he can hoe, hoe, hoe.

What is a parent's favorite Christmas carol?

Silent Night.

Why is it cold on Christmas Day?

Because it's in Decembrrrrrr.

ANIMAL ANTICS...
AGAIN

Why did the pig become an actor?

Because he was a ham.

How do you save a deer during hunting season?

You hang on for deer life.

When does a dog go "moo"?

When it is learning a new language.

Why do seagulls fly over the sea?

> *Because if they flew over the bay,
> they would be bagels.*

What kind of pigs know karate?

> *Pork chops.*

Who stole the soap?

> *The robber ducky.*

What do you call a happy Lassie?

> *A jolly collie.*

How do Hispanic sheep say
Merry Christmas?

> *Fleece Navidad.*

What kind of ties do pigs wear?

> *Pigs-ties.*

Where does a peacock go when it loses its tail?

A re-tail store.

What's worse than raining cats and dogs?

Hailing taxis.

What kind of cats like to go bowling?

Alley cats.

Why did the pig take a bath?

The farmer said, "Hogwash."

What do you call a deer with no eyes?

I have no I-deer.

What do you call a deer with no eyes and no legs?

Still no eye-deer.

Why does a flamingo stand on one leg?

Because if he lifted that leg off the ground, he would fall down.

How did the little Scottish dog feel when he saw a monster?

He was terrier-fied.

What do ducks watch on TV?

Duckumentaries.

How many sheep does it take to knit a sweater?

Don't be silly; sheep can't knit.

What do you call cattle with a sense of humor?

Laughing stock.

Why don't sharks like fast food?

Because they can't catch it.

What do you get if you cross a frog
and a dog?

A croaker spaniel.

What animal sounds like a sheep
but isn't?

A baaaa-boon.

Where do Eskimos train their dogs?

In the mush room.

Why was the sheep pulled over
on the freeway?

Because she did a ewe-turn.

What did the shark say to the whale?

"What are you blubbering about?"

How do monkeys get down the stairs?

They slide down the bananaster.

What do you get if you cross an angry sheep and a grumpy cow?

An animal that's in a baaaaaaad mooooooood.

What is a frog's favorite hot drink?

Hot croak-o.

How do chickens bake a cake?

From scratch.

What do you give a sick pig?

Oinkment.

What is a cat's favorite song?

Three Blind Mice.

What dog loves to take bubble baths?

A shampoodle.

Why are elephants so poor?

Because they work for peanuts.

What did the doctor say when the monkey cut off his tail?

"It won't be long now."

What do you call a cow with two legs?

Lean beef.

What do you call a cow with no legs?

Ground beef.

What goes dot-dot-croak, dot-dash-croak?

A morse toad.

What's black and white, black and white, and black and white?

A panda bear rolling down a hill.

What do you call a fish without an eye?

A fsh.

What do you call a snake with a great personality?

A snake charmer.

Why did the piece of gum cross the road?

It was stuck to the chicken's foot.

What do you get if you cross a cocker spaniel, a poodle, and a rooster?

Cockerpoodledoo.

If fruit comes from a fruit tree, where does chicken come from?

A poul-tree.

Where do frogs leave their hats
and coats?

In the croakroom.

How do you stop an elephant
from charging?

Take away its credit card.

MEDICAL MISCHIEF

Why did the bee go to the doctor?

Because it had hives.

What does a dentist call his X-rays?

Tooth-pics.

What does a sick lemon need?

Lemon aid.

What does a doctor give an elephant who's going to be sick?

Plenty of room.

Why didn't the girl tell the doctor that she ate some glue?

Her lips were sealed.

What did the nose say to the finger?

"Stop picking on me."

What do you give a dog with a fever?

Ketchup. It's the best thing for a hot dog.

Why did the banana go to the doctor?

It was not peeling well.

Why did the boy tiptoe past the medicine cabinet?

He didn't want to wake the sleeping pills.

What kind of button won't unbutton?

A bellybutton.

When is the best time to go
to the dentist?

At tooth-hurty.

Why did the computer go
to the doctor?

Because it had a virus.

What did one eyeball say
to the other eyeball?

*"Between you and me
something smells."*

Why did the cookie go to the hospital?

He felt crummy.

What is a happy doctor's favorite
blood type?

B positive.

What did the judge say to the dentist?

"Do you swear to pull the tooth, the whole tooth, and nothing but the tooth?"

Why did the king go to the dentist?

To get his teeth crowned.

What does a dentist do during an earthquake?

He braces himself.

What did the tooth say to the dentist as she was leaving?

"Fill me in when you get back."

What is a dentist's favorite animal?

A molar bear.

Has your tooth stopped hurting yet?

I don't know, the dentist kept it.

What did the dentist get for an award?

A little plaque.

When does a doctor get mad?

When he runs out of patients.

Why did the pillow go to the doctor?

He was feeling all stuffed up.

Where does a boat go when it's sick?

To the dock.

What did one tonsil say
to the other tonsil?

*"Get dressed up; the doctor
is taking us out."*

Patient: Doctor, sometimes I feel like I'm invisible.

Doctor: Who said that?

Patient: Doctor, Doctor I think I'm a moth.

Doctor: Get out of my light.

Patient: Doctor, I keep hearing a ringing sound.

Doctor: Then answer the phone.

Did you hear the one about the germ?

Never mind, I don't want to spread it around.

How do you cure a headache?

Put your head through a window and the pane will disappear.

LEGAL LAUGHS

What did the judge say when the skunk walked in the court room?

"Odor in the court."

What do prisoners use to call each other?

Cellphones.

What do lawyers wear to court?

Lawsuits.

Why did the picture go to jail?

Because it was framed.

What four letters will frighten a burglar?

O I C U.

What is it that even the most careful lawyers overlook?

Their nose.

Did you hear about the robbery last night?

Two clothes pins held up a sweater.

What do you call an underwater spy?

James Pond.

What did the lawyer name his daughter?

Sue.

Why did the policeman go to the baseball game?

He heard someone had stolen a base.

Why did the book join the police?

He wanted to go undercover.

What do you get a man who has everything for his birthday?

A burglar alarm.

Why was the belt arrested?

Because it held up some pants.

KNOCK KNOCK JOKES

Knock, knock.

Who's there?

Cows go.

Cows go who?

No, cows go moo.

Knock, knock.

Who's there?

Mary.

Mary who?

Marry me?

Knock, knock.

Who's there?

Nerf.

Nerf who?

Your nephew.

Knock, knock.

Who's there?

Heart.

Heart who?

Heart to hear you. Can you speak up?

Knock, knock.

Who's there?

Honey.

Honey who?

Honey, I'm home.

Knock, knock.

Who's there?

Me.

Me, who?

You don't know who you are?

Knock, knock.

Who's there?

Ice cream.

Ice cream who?

Ice cream if you don't let me in.

Knock, knock.

Who's there?

Pecan.

Pecan who?

Pecan someone your own size.

Knock, knock.

Who's there?

Bison.

Bison who?

Bison girl scout cookies.

Knock, knock.

Who's there?

Water.

Water who?

Water way to answer the door.

Knock, knock.

Who's there?

Pudding.

Pudding who?

Pudding your shoes on before your pants is a silly idea.

Knock, knock.

Who's there?

Ketchup.

Ketchup who?

Ketchup to me and I will tell you.

Knock, knock.

Who's there?

Orange.

Orange who?

Orange you going to answer the door?

Knock, knock.

Who's there?

Beets.

Beets who?

Beets me.

Knock, knock.

Who's there?

Water.

Water who?

*Water those plants
or they're going to die.*

Knock, knock.

Who's there?

Closure.

Closure who?

Closure mouth while you're eating, please.

Knock, knock.

Who's there?

Sultan.

Sultan who?

Sultan pepper.

Knock, knock.

Who's there?

Two fours.

Two fours who?

No need to make lunch we already 8.

Knock, knock.

Who's there?

Imani.

Imani who?

Imani pickle, open the door.

Knock, knock.

Who's there?

Sweden.

Sweden who?

*Sweden the coffee
and open the door.*

Knock, knock.

Who's there?

Muffin.

Muffin who?

*Muffin the matter with me,
how about you?*

Knock, knock.

Who's there?

Turnip.

Turnip who?

*Turnip the volume,
it's my favorite song.*

Knock, knock.

Who's there?

Lettuce.

Lettuce who?

Lettuce in; it's cold.

Knock, knock.

Who's there?

Olive.

Olive who?

Olive you.

Knock, knock.

Who's there?

Omelet.

Omelet who?

Omelet smarter than I look.

Knock, knock.

Who's there?

Doughnut.

Doughnut who?

Doughnut disturb me.

Knock, knock.

Who's there?

Cash.

Cash who?

No thanks, but I'd like some peanuts.

Knock, knock.

Who's there?

Candy.

Candy who?

Candy cow jump over the moon?

Knock, knock.

Who's there?

Carrot.

Carrot who?

Do you even carrot all?

Knock, knock.

Who's there?

Celery.

Celery who?

Celery isn't high enough. I quit.

Knock, knock.

Who's there?

Pasta.

Pasta who?

Pasta la vista baby.

Knock, knock.

Who's there?

Eggs.

Eggs who?

Eggcited to meet you.

Knock, knock.

Who's there?

Broccoli.

Broccoli who?

*Broccoli doesn't have
a last name, silly.*

Knock, knock.

Who's there?

Noah.

Noah who?

Noah good place to eat?

Knock, knock.

Who's there?

Cook.

Cook who?

Hey, I'm not crazy.

Knock, knock.

Who's there?

Isma.

Isma who?

Isma lunch ready yet?

Knock, knock.

Who's there?

Butter.

Butter who?

Butter tell you a few more knock knock jokes.

Knock, knock.

Who's there?

Stopwatch.

Stopwatch who?

*Stopwatch your doing
and open the door.*

Knock, knock.

Who's there?

Wire.

Wire who?

Wire you asking; I just told you.

Knock, knock.

Who's there?

Cotton.

Cotton who?

Cotton a trap, can you help me out?

Knock, knock.

Who's there?

See.

See who?

See you, if you'll let me in.

Knock, knock.

Who's there?

Alexia.

Alexia who?

Alexia again to open this door.

Knock, knock.

Who's there?

Toby.

Toby who?

Toby or not Toby;
that is the question.

Knock, knock.

Who's there?

Abby.

Abby who?

Abby birthday to you.

Knock, knock.

Who's there?

Adolph.

Adolph who?

Adolph ball hit me in the mouth.

Knock, knock.

Who's there?

Aida.

Aida who?

*Aida lot of sweets
and now I've got tummy ache.*

Knock, knock.

Who's there?

Al.

Al who?

*Al give you a hug
if you open this door.*

Knock, knock.

Who's there?

Aladdin.

Aladdin who?

*Aladdin the street wants
a word with you.*

Knock, knock.

Who's there?

Aldo.

Aldo who?

Aldo anywhere with you.

Knock, knock.

Who's there?

Alec.

Alec who?

Alec-tricity. Isn't that a shock?

Knock, knock.

Who's there?

Alex.

Alex who?

Alex-plain later; let me in!

Knock, knock.

Who's there?

Anna.

Anna who?

Anna going to tell you.

Knock, knock.

Who's there?

Avery.

Avery who?

Avery thing but the kitchen sink.

Knock, knock.

Who's there?

Justin.

Justin who?

Just in time for dinner.

Knock, knock.

Who's there?

Rita.

Rita who?

Rita a little more and you'll find out.

Knock, knock.

Who's there?

Owl.

Owl who?

Owl aboard.

Knock, knock.

Who's there?

Chimp.

Chimp who?

I think it's pronounced shampoo.

WELL THAT'S PUNNY

Pencils could be made with erasers at both ends...

but what would be the point?

I was struggling to figure out how lightning works...

then it struck me.

She broke her finger today...

but on the other hand she was completely fine.

I've just been on a once-in-a-lifetime holiday.

I'll tell you what, never again.

Some people say I'm addicted to somersaults...

but that's just how I roll.

Never lie to an x-ray technician.

They can see right through you.

My friend made a joke about a TV controller.

It wasn't remotely funny.

I have a speed bump phobia...

but I'm slowly getting over it.

I'm working on a device that will read minds.

I'd love to hear your thoughts.

I saw an ad that read: Television for free, volume stuck on full.

I thought to myself, I can't turn that down.

I thought about becoming a wizard...

so I tried it for a spell.

I got one of those new corduroy pillows.

They are making headlines.

I get paid to sleep.

It's a dream job.

I went to a restaurant last night and had the Wookie steak.

It was a little Chewy.

I have some broken puppets for sale.

No strings attached.

When it came to getting even with my local bus company...

I pulled out all the stops.

I find the best way to communicate with fish...

is to drop them a line.

My friend's bakery burned down last night.

Now his business is toast.

A man just hit me with milk, cream, and butter.

How dairy.

I used to have a fear of hurdles...

but I got over it.

Inspecting mirrors is a job I could...

really see myself doing.

Someone just stole my mood ring.

I'm not sure how I feel about that.

I never trust atoms.

They make up everything.

I can't believe I got fired from the calendar factory.

All I did was take a day off.

I was going to buy a book on phobias...

but I was afraid it wouldn't help me.

I can hear music coming out of my printer.

I think the paper's jammin' again.

Yesterday, I accidentally swallowed some food coloring.

The doctor says I'm okay...
but I feel like I've dyed a little inside.

Wind turbines.

I'm a big fan.

It's really difficult to find what you want on eBay.

I was searching for fire starters and found over 15,000 matches.

I don't trust these stairs...

they're always up to something.

I had a neck brace fitted years ago.

I've never looked back since.

My time machine and I...

go way back.

My fear of moving stairs...

is escalating.

I used to be a train driver...

but I got sidetracked.

I left my friend because she wouldn't stop counting.

I wonder what she's up to now.

My sister bet me $100 that I couldn't build a working car out of spaghetti.

You should've seen her face as I drove pasta.

I did a theatrical performance about puns.

Really it was just a play on words.

My mom just found out that I replaced her bed with a trampoline.

She hit the roof.

Singing in the shower is all fun and games until you get shampoo in your mouth.

Then it becomes a soap opera.

I know how batteries feel.

I'm not included in most things either.

I heard a funny joke about a boomerang earlier.

I'm sure it'll come back to me eventually.

I asked the lion in my wardrobe what he was doing there;

he said it was "Narnia Business."

I tried to catch some fog.

I mist.

I knew a couple who met in a revolving door.

*I think they're still
going around together.*

I woke up this morning and forgot which side the sun rises from.

Then it dawned on me.

I'm very good friends with 25 letters of the alphabet.

I don't know y.

DID YOU KNOW...

Jokes about German sausages are the wurst.

The person who invented the door knock won the No-bell prize.

Taller people sleep longer in a bed?

A golf ball is a golf ball no matter how you putt it.

Never give your uncle an anteater.

Whiteboards are remarkable.

Regular visitors to the dentist are familiar with the drill.

Reading while sunbathing makes you well red.

A chicken crossing the road is poultry in motion.

Claustrophobic people are more productive thinking outside of the box.

Insect puns bug people.

Shout out to everyone wondering what the opposite of "in" is.

Time flies like an arrow. Fruit flies like a banana.

Two antennas met, fell in love, and eventually got married.

The wedding ceremony wasn't much, but the reception was excellent.

A small boy swallowed some coins and was taken to the hospital.
When his grandmother telephoned to ask how he was, the nurse said,

"No change yet."

Did you hear about the guy who got hit in the head with a can of soda?

He was lucky it was a soft drink.

Did you hear about the girl whose whole left side was missing?

She's all right now.

TRICKY TITLES

I Win

   by U. Lose

Robots

   by Anne Droid

Danger!

   by Luke Out

Cloning

   by Irma Dubble II

Hot Dog
>by Frank Furter

I'm Fine
>by Howard Yu

I'm Smarter
>by Gene Yuss

Downpour
>by Wayne Dwops

Sea Birds
>by Al Batross

Teach Me
>by I. Wanda Know

I Say So

by Frank O. Pinion

Tug of War

by Paul Harder

Surprised

by Omar Goodness

Good Works

by Ben Evolent

April Fools

by Sue Prize

Come On In

by Doris Open

Get Moving!

　　by Sheik Aleg

I Like Fish

　　by Ann Chovie

May Flowers

　　by April Showers

Pain Relief

　　by Ann L. Gesick

It's Unfair

　　by Y. Me

How to Annoy

　　by Aunt Agonize

40-Love

    by Dennis Court

The Roof Has a Hole

    by Lee King

African Safari

    by L.A. Funt

Ten Years in the Bathtub

    by Ima Prune

I Don't Smell Good

    by Anita Bath

The Art of Being Discreet

    by Anonymous

101 Ways to Diet
    by I. M. Hungry

More Green Vegetables
    by Broke Ali

Don't Raise Your Arms
    by Harry Pitts

Sitting on the Beach
    by Sandy Bottom

Window Coverings
    by Kurt and Rod

How to Get Good Grades
    by Samar T. Pants

The Skyline
by Bill Ding

Ouch!
by A. B. Sting

Helping Out
by Abel N. Willing

I Love You!
By Alma Heart

It Blew Off My Hat
by Augusta Wind

I Shoot Arrows
by Anne Archer

Not Optional
   by Amanda Tory

Not A Cello
   by Amanda Linn

What's for Dinner?
   by Amelia Eat

Types of Birds
   by A. V. Airy

How to Make Honey
   by A. Beeman

Who Killed the Woodpecker?
   by B. B. Gunn

How to Make Money
    by Mell Yenere

Lucky As Can Be
    by Bess Twishes

Sandwiches
    by B. L. Tea

I Always Smell
    by B. O. Issues

Stay Away
    by Barb Dwire

Top Signs
    by Bill Board

Let's Grill

by Barb E. Que

Fun Party Ideas

by Bobby Frapples

Haircuts

by Buz Cutt

Feelings

by Cara Lot

Suppertime

by Cam N. Getit

Dinosaurs that Eat Meat

by Carn E. Vores

Lovely Jewels

by Cristal Myne

How to Cook Bacon

by Chris P. Swine

Music for Children

by Zy L'fon

Rocket Launching

by Leif Toff

Poor Sportsmanship

by Collet Quits

A Day off Work

by Collin Sic

Chores

by Dustin Klean

Twelve Months

by Dee Cember

Making Decisions

by D. Side

Rats in the House

by E. E. K. Mouse

Make Money Fast

by E. Z. Cashe

Fun in the Sky

by Ella Copter

Drawing Tips
by Illis Traight

Full Tires
by Erin Side

She Sees Him
by Esau Hurr

Framed
by Gil T.

Pop History
by Ginger Ale

After Work
by Gwen Hom

Rapunzel Stories
   by Harris Long

No Camels in the Zoo
   by Humphrey Space

Delicious Breakfast Foods
   by Hamm N. Eggs

Vegetarian Dinosaurs
   by Herb A. Vore

His Girl Thursday
   by Herman Friday

Comedians
   by Hillary Uss

Being a Jockey
by Hors Ryder

Need for a Recipe
by Ingrid E. Ants

The Post Office
by Imelda Letter

Planning a Surprise
by Izzy Backyet

The First Month
by Jan Yuary

Lots of Colors
by Jason Rainbows

How Airplanes Run
   by Jett Fuel

Where to Work Out
   by Jim Nasium

Don't Stop Believing
   by Kerry Onn

We're Almost There
   by Knot Quite

Honest People
   by Laura Byder

Ballet
   by Leah Tard

Help Out

by Linda Hand

It's Fall

by Leif Raker

Don't Be Greedy

by Les Ismoore

Hawaiian Parties

by Lou Wow

Speak Up

by Louden Clear

We're Not All Winners

by Lou Zer

How to Behave
    by B. Morell

Kings and Queens Rule
    by M. Pyres

The Perfect Ingredient
    by May O'Naze

The Best Thing on Pancakes
    by Mable Syrup

Favorite Dinners for Kids
    by Mack Aroni

Computer Won't Work
    by Mel Function

All in Your Head
   by Mag Ination

Failing Classes
   by Milo Grades

Where to Park a Boat
   by Marina Dock

Not Brand New
   by Mark Dupp

Karate
   by Marsha Larts

Fire Me Up
   by Matt Chez

Works of God
  by Mira Q. Luss

You're Silly
  by Noah Fence

The Flood
  by Noah S. Arc

Playing Bridge
  by Paco Cards

How to Read a Book
  by Paige Turner

On a Budget
  by Penny Pincher

ROFL RIDDLES

A king, queen, and twins are in a room. How are there no people in the room?

They are beds.

A mirror for the famous, but informative to all. I'll show you the world, but it might be a bit small.

What am I?

A television.

How can you throw a ball 20 feet and have it come back to you without hitting anything?

Throw it up in the air.

What three positive numbers equal the same number when added or multiplied together?

1, 2, and 3.

There is a stone stove and a brick stove. You only have one match.

What do you light up first?

The match.

I have no wallet, but I pay my way.
I travel the world, but in the corner I stay.

What am I?

A stamp.

Jack's mother has three kids. April is the first one. May is the second child.

What's the third child's name?

Jack.

The dirtier I am, the whiter I get. You leave a mark on me when you stand, and I'll leave a mark on you when you sit.

What am I?

A chalkboard.

What occurs once in a minute, twice in a moment, but never in a thousand years?

The letter M.

You use me from your head to your toes; the more you use me the thinner I grow.

What am I?

A bar of soap.

What starts with e, but only has one letter in it?

An envelope.

When you need me, you throw me away.
When you don't, you bring me back.

What am I?

An anchor.

What has to be broken before you can
use it?

An egg.

What is the easiest way to poke a
balloon without popping it?

Do it when it's not blown up.

I have every color, but no gold.

What am I?

A rainbow.

What is as old as the earth, but new
every month?

The moon.

I fly, but I have no wings. I cry, but I have no eyes.

What am I?

A cloud.

Poor people have it. Rich people need it. If you eat it you die.

What is it?

Nothing.

100 feet in the air, but its back is on the ground.

What is it?

A centipede.

How do you make the number one disappear?

Add a g to it, and it's gone.

Give me food and I will live, feed me water and I'll die.

What am I?

A fire.

The blue man lives in the blue house. The green man lives in the green house.

Who lives in the white house?

The president.

I'm tall when I'm young, and I'm short when I'm old.

What am I?

A candle.

I am an odd number, take away one letter and I become even.

What number am I?

Seven. If you take away the s, seven becomes even.

What starts with the letter T, is filled with T, and ends with the letter T?

A teapot.

There are three apples and you take away two.

How many apples do you have?

You took two, so of course you have two.

A boy fell off a 30-foot ladder, but didn't get hurt.

How is this possible?

He only fell off the first step.

The more you take, the more you leave behind.

What are they?

Footprints.

Imagine you're in a room with no windows or doors and it's filling with water.

What do you do?

Stop imagining.

At night they appear, but during the day they're lost.

What are they?

Stars.

What is black when you buy it, red when you use it, and gray when you throw it away?

Charcoal.

What is the best way to stop a dog from digging holes in the front yard?

Put it in the backyard.

What's the easiest way to double your money?

Hold it in front of the mirror.

What can be broken without being held?

A promise.

If an electric train is going south, which way is the smoke blowing?

An electric train doesn't have any smoke.

How can a pants pocket be empty and still have something in it?

It can have a hole in it.

What belongs to you, but others use it more than you do?

Your name.

A rooster lays an egg at six in the morning.

When does the farmer find it?

Never. A rooster doesn't lay eggs.

How many eggs can you put in an empty basket?

Only one, because after that, it's not empty.

What's the longest word in the dictionary?

Smiles, because there's a mile between each S.

If you look at my face, there won't be thirteen in any place.

What am I?

A clock.

Everyone has me, but can't get rid of me.

What am I?

> *A shadow.*

I'm heavy, but not backwards.

What am I?

> *The word "ton."*

I brighten your day,
but I live in the shade.

What am I?

> *A lamp.*

Who gets paid when they drive away
their customers?

> *A taxi driver.*

A man shaves many times in one day, but still has a very long beard.

How does this happen?

He is a barber.

I don't eat food, but I enjoy a light meal every day.

What am I?

A plant.

I run around the house, but I don't move.

What am I?

A fence.

I have 88 keys, but can't open a door.

What am I?

A piano.

I have a foot but no leg.

What am I?

A ruler.

I'm round at the ends
and high in the middle.

What am I?

Ohio.

I have three letters and start with gas.

What am I?

A car.

I have a hand and fingers
but I am not alive.

What am I?

A glove.

What's always coming, but never arrives?

Tomorrow.

I never ask questions
but often get answered.

What am I?

A doorbell.

I can be caught but not thrown.

What am I?

A cold.

I have three feet but cannot walk.

What am I?

A yard stick.

TASTY TONGUE TWISTERS

I saw a saw that could out saw
any other saw I ever saw.

A big bug bit the little beetle but
the little beetle bit the big bug back.

Six slippery snails, slid slowly seaward.

How much wood could a wood chuck
chuck if a wood chuck could chuck wood.

Any noise annoys an oyster but
a noisy noise annoys an oyster more.

Fuzzy wuzzy was a bear.
Fuzzy wuzzy had no hair.
Fuzzy wuzzy wasn't fuzzy... was he?

If a black bug bleeds black blood,
what color blood does a blue bug bleed?

Crisp crusts crackle and crunch.

Round the rugged rocks
the ragged rascals ran.

Growing gray goats graze great green
grassy groves.

Which wrist watches
are Swiss wrist watches?

Fred fed Ted bread
and Ted fed Fred bread.

I scream, you scream,
we all scream for ice cream.

Four furious friends fought for the phone.

The cat catchers can't catch caught cats.

Three fluffy feathers fell from Fanny's flimsy fan.

Rory's lawn rake rarely rakes really right.

Toy boat. Toy boat. Toy boat.

She should shun the shining sun.

Cooks cook cupcakes quickly.

She sold six shabby sheared sheep.

Mix a box of mixed biscuits
with a boxed biscuit mixer.

Twelve twins twirled twelve twigs.

If you notice this notice, you will notice that this notice is not worth noticing.

The bottom of the butter bucket is the buttered bucket bottom.

Five frantic frogs fled from fifty fierce fish.

Betty and Bob brought back blue balloons from the big bazaar.

Little Lillian lets lazy lizards lie along the lily pads.

Does your sport shop stock short socks with spots?

Many mumbling mice are making merry music in the moonlight.

The boot black brought
the black boot back.

A synonym for cinnamon is a cinnamon
synonym.

The great Greek grape growers grow
great Greek grapes.

No need to light a nightlight on a light
night like tonight.

Green glass globes glow greenly.

Clean clams crammed in clean cans.

A slimy snake slithered
down the sandy Sahara.

She sees cheese.

Bake big batches of bitter brown bread.

Six socks sit in a sink,
soaking in soap suds.

Shave a single shingle thin.

She sells sea shells by the sea shore.

Shun the sunshine.

I wish to wish the wish you wish to wish.

A flea and a fly in a flue.

Fred fried fresh fruit on Friday.

THE GREAT OUTDOORS

What language does a billboard speak?

Sign language.

Does Canaada have a 4th of July?

Yes, right after the 3rd of July.

What is at the end of the rainbow?

The letter "w."

What's purple and 5,000 miles long?

The Grape Wall of China.

What did the red light
say to the green light?

Don't look, I'm changing.

What do you get when you pour
cement on a burglar?

A hardened criminal.

What do you call a knight
who is afraid to fight?

Sir Render.

What happens when you throw a red
rock into a blue sea?

It sinks.

Why don't mountains catch colds?

They have snow caps!

LITERALLY. BEST. JOKES. EVER.

JOKES for KIDS

CHANTELLE GRACE

WHO'S THERE?

Knock, knock.

Who's there?

Avery.

Avery who?

Avery time I come to your house we go through this.

Knock, knock.

Who's there?

Goat.

Goat who?

Goat on a limb and open the door.

Knock, knock.

Who's there?

Lion.

Lion who?

Lion on your doorstep; open up.

Knock, knock.

Who's there?

Dragon.

Dragon who?

Dragon your feet again.

Knock, knock.

Who's there?

Duck.

Duck who?

Just duck!
They're throwing things at us.

Knock, knock.

Who's there?

Toucan.

Toucan who?

Toucan play that game.

Knock, knock.

Who's there?

Wood ant.

Wood ant who?

Don't be afraid. Wood ant harm a fly.

Knock, knock.

Who's there?

Owl.

Owl who?

*Owl good things come
to those who wait.*

Knock, knock.

Who's there?

Safari.

Safari who?

Safari so good.

Knock, knock.

Who's there?

Fleas.

Fleas who?

Fleas a jolly good fellow.

Knock, knock.

Who's there?

Nana.

Nana who?

Nana your business.

Knock, knock.

Who's there?

Laughing tentacles.

Laughing tentacles who?

*You would laugh too,
if you had tentacles.*

Knock, knock.

Who's there?

Cracker.

Cracker who?

*Cracker another bad joke
and I'm leaving.*

Knock, knock.

Who's there?

Honey bee.

Honey bee who?

Honey, be a doll and open the door.

Knock, knock.

Who's there?

Duncan.

Duncan who?

Duncan my cookies in milk.
Can you open the door?

Knock, knock.

Who's there?

Rhino.

Rhino who?

Rhino every knock knock joke there is.

Knock, knock.

Who's there?

Rabbit.

Rabbit who?

Rabbit up carefully; it's fragile.

Knock, knock.

Who's there?

Herd.

Herd who?

Herd you were home, so can you come out?

Knock, knock.

Who's there?

Bee.

Bee who?

Bee at my house at hive-o-clock.

Knock, knock.

Who's there?

Ya.

Ya who?

Actually, I prefer Google.

Knock, knock.

Who's there?

Gorilla.

Gorilla who?

Gorilla me a hamburger, please.

Knock, knock.

Who's there?

Roof.

Roof who?

Roof day. Let me in.

Knock, knock.

Who's there?

Whale.

Whale who?

*Whale, whale, whale,
what do we have here?*

Knock, knock.

Who's there?

Chimp.

Chimp who?

Chimp off the old block.

Knock, knock.

Who's there?

Iguana.

Iguana who?

Iguana hold your hand.

Knock, knock.

Who's there?

Herring.

Herring who?

*Herring some awful
knock-knock jokes.*

Knock, knock.

Who's there?

Sore ewe.

Sore ewe who?

*Sore ewe gonna open
the door or not?*

Knock, knock.

Who's there?

Geese.

Geese who?

Geese what I'm going to do if you don't open the door.

Knock, knock.

Who's there?

Alligator.

Alligator who?

Alligator for her birthday was a card.

Knock, knock.

Who's there?

Bat.

Bat who?

Bat you'll never guess.

Knock, knock.

Who's there?

Howl.

Howl who?

*Howl you know unless
you open the door.*

Knock, knock.

Who's there?

Fangs.

Fangs who?

Fangs for letting me in.

Knock, knock.

Who's there?

Thumping.

Thumping who?

Thumping green and slimy is climbing up your back.

Knock, knock.

Who's there?

Teddy.

Teddy who?

*Teddy is the beginning
of the rest of your life.*

Why did the chicken cross the road?

To get to your house.

Knock, knock.

Who's there?

The chicken.

Knock, knock.

Who's there?

Odysseus.

Odysseus who?

Odysseus the last straw.

Knock, knock.

Who's there?

You know.

You know who?

Exactly.

Knock, knock.

Who's there?

Wendy.

Wendy who?

*Wendy wind blows
it messes up my hair.*

Knock, knock.

Who's there?

Barbara.

Barbara who?

*Barbara black sheep
have you any wool?*

Knock, knock.

Who's there?

Theresa.

Theresa who?

Theresa joke for everyone.

Knock, knock.

Who's there?

Horton hears a.

Horton hears a who?

I didn't know you liked Dr. Seuss.

Knock, knock.

Who's there?

Rita.

Rita who?

Rita book of knock knock jokes.

Knock, knock.

Who's there?

Butter.

Butter who?

Butter if you don't know.

Knock, knock.

Who's there?

Alex.

Alex who?

Alex the questions around here.

Knock, knock.

Who's there?

Lettuce.

Lettuce who?

Lettuce in and you'll find out.

Knock, knock.

Who's there?

Abbey.

Abbey who?

Abbey stung me on the arm.

Knock, knock.

Who's there?

Rhoda.

Rhoda who?

*Rhoda long way to get here;
now open up.*

Knock, knock.

Who's there?

I'm T.

I'm T who?

Oh, you're only 2?
Is your mom home?

Knock, knock.

Who's there?

Well not your parents
because they don't knock.

PUN FUN

I'm taking part in a stair climbing competition.

Guess I better step up my game.

My first job was working in an orange juice factory.

I got canned: couldn't concentrate.

A friend of mine tried to annoy me with bird puns...

but I soon realized that toucan play that game.

I used to be a banker...

but then I lost interest.

I'm reading a book about anti-gravity.

It's impossible to put down.

I'd tell you a chemistry joke...

but I know I wouldn't get a reaction.

I relish the fact that you've mustard
the strength to ketchup to me.

Without geometry...

life is pointless.

I went to a seafood disco last week...

and pulled a mussel.

She had a photographic memory...

but never developed it.

Don't spell part backwards.

It's a trap.

A boiled egg every morning...

is hard to beat.

Let's talk about rights and lefts.

You were right, so I left.

In the winter my dog wears his coat...

*but in the summer
he wears his coat and pants.*

A skunk fell in the river...

and stank to the bottom.

A new type of broom has come out.

It is sweeping the nation.

My friend asked me to stop impersonating a flamingo.

I had to put my foot down.

Someone ripped some pages out of both ends of my dictionary today.

It just goes from bad to worse.

I used to be a baker...

but I didn't make enough dough.

The first time I got a universal remote control I thought to myself...

"This changes everything."

I haven't slept for ten days.

That would be far too long.

I've just written a song about tortillas.

Actually, it's more of a rap.

A book just fell on my head.

I've only got my shelf to blame.

Someone threw cheese at me.

Real mature!

I love Switzerland.

I'm not sure what the best thing about it is, but their flag is a big plus.

When I finally worked out the secret to cloning...

I was beside myself.

A pet store had a bird contest...

with no perches necessary.

I wondered why the ball
kept getting bigger.

Then it hit me.

The other day a clown held the door
open for me.

I thought it was a nice jester.

I asked my mom to make me a pair of
pants.

She was happy to.
Or at least sew it seams.

I applied for a job at the local restaurant.

I'm still waiting.

I was going to look for my missing watch...

but I could never find the time.

I've been learning braille.

I'm sure I'll master it once I get a feel for it.

If a judge loves the sound of his own voice...

expect a long sentence.

I just walked past a shop that was giving out dead batteries...

free of charge.

I used to be addicted to soap...

but I'm clean now.

It was an emotional wedding.

Even the cake was in tiers.

Once you've seen one shopping center...

you've seen a mall.

The other day someone left a piece of clay in my house.

I didn't know what to make of it.

I'd tell you my construction joke...

but I'm still working on it.

My grandma is having trouble with her new stair lift.

It's driving her up the wall.

To the guy who invented zero:

Thanks for nothing.

There was a big paddle sale at the boat store.

It was quite an oar deal.

I tried to finish the left-overs...

but... foiled again.

I really wanted camouflage socks...

but I couldn't find any.

I couldn't work out how to fasten my seatbelt.

Then it clicked.

Did you hear about those new reversible jackets?

I'm excited to see how they turn out.

I'm glad I know sign language.

It's pretty handy.

My dog can do magic tricks.

It's a labracadabrador.

Learning how to collect trash wasn't that hard.

I just picked it up as I went along.

My leaf blower doesn't work.

It sucks.

If you need help building an ark...

I Noah guy.

This boy said he was going to hit me with the neck of a guitar.

I said, "Is that a fret?"

RAD RIDDLES

I'm light as a feather, but even the strongest man cannot hold me for more than five minutes.

What am I?

Breath.

Mr. Smith has two children. If one of the children is a boy, what are the chances the other is a boy?

50%.

When is homework not homework?

When you do it at school.

What stays put when it goes off?

An alarm clock.

Alexa gets into the shower, gets out, and realizes her hair isn't wet.

How is this possible?

She didn't turn on the water.

What is sticky and brown?

A stick.

What are two things you can't eat for breakfast?

Lunch and dinner.

Without fingers, I point.
Without feet, I run.

What am I?

A clock.

Is an older one-hundred dollar bill worth more than a newer one?

Of course it is. A $100 bill is worth more than a $1 bill.

You throw away the outside, eat the middle, and throw away the inside.

What is it?

Corn on the cob.

I am an instrument that you can hear, but cannot see or touch.

What am I?

A voice.

Two people were born in the moment, but have different birthdays.

How does this happen?

They were born in different time zones.

I can be used to build castles,
but I crumble in your hands.

What am I?

Sand.

I'm in everybody, but everyone still
wants me. I can't feed you,
but I can feed a tree.

What am I?

Water.

A cowboy rode to an inn on Friday.
He stayed two days and left on Friday.

How is this possible?

His horse's name was Friday.

You can easily touch me, but not see
me. You can throw me out, but not
throw me away.

What am I?

Your back.

If you're looking for some food, I know what to do. But if you don't like the cold, I'm not for you.

What am I?

A fridge.

You are my brother, but I am not yours.

Who am I?

Your sister.

What kind of room has no windows or doors?

A mushroom.

The more you work, the more I eat. You keep me full, I'll keep you neat!

What am I?

A pencil sharpener.

I'm very easy to get into,
but very hard to get out of.

What am I?

Trouble.

A man is sitting in a cabin in Michigan.
Three hours later he gets out of his
cabin in Texas.

How is this possible?

He's a pilot in the cabin of a plane.

If a white house is white and a yellow
house is yellow, what color is a green
house?

*A greenhouse is one that holds
plants; it's usually clear.*

Can you name three consecutive days without using the words Wednesday, Friday, or Sunday?

Yesterday, today, and tomorrow.

I bring you down but never up.

What am I?

Gravity.

Two fish are in a tank.
One says to the other,

"Err... so how do you drive this thing?"

A man is twenty years old,
but has had only five birthdays.

Why?

He was born on Leap Year Day.

What month do people sleep the least?

February, because it's the shortest month.

How many apples grow on a tree?

All apples grow on trees.

What has a single eye, but cannot see?

A needle.

THINK ABOUT IT...

If you're waiting for the waiter to bring you food,

are you the waiter?

If a dog gave birth to puppies near the road,

would it get a ticket for littering?

If you dream in color,

is it a pigment of your imagination?

If a clock is hungry,

does it go back four seconds?

If you crash a car on purpose,

is it still an accident?

Why do noses run,

but feet smell?

Is sand called sand because

it's between the sea and the land?

If we can't see air,

do fish see water?

If I hit myself and it hurts,

am I weak or strong?

If I work as Security at the Samsung store,

does that make me guardian of the galaxy?

Why are they called apartments

if they are built together?

Who put the alphabet

in alphabetical order?

If a dog chews shoes

whose shoes does he choose?

Would a cardboard belt

be a waist of paper?

TITLE TREATS

I Love Wills
 by Benny Fishery

Stop Arguing
 by Xavier Breath

Falling Trees
 by Tim Burr

Monkeys
 by Bob Boone

Why Cars Stop
   by M.T. Tank

Turtle Racing
   by Eubie Quick

I Love Crowds
   by Morris Merrier

The Yellow River
   by I. P. Freely

A Great Plenty
   by E. Nuff

Mosquito Bites
   by Ivan Itch

My Lost Causes
   by Noah Veil

Flooring
   by Lynn O'Leum

It's a Shocker
   by Alec Tricity

I Hit the Wall
   by Isadore There

I Hate the Sun
   by Gladys Knight

He Disappeared
   by Otto Sight

I Didn't Do It!
   by Ivan Alibi

Life in Chicago
   by Wendy City

Without Warning
   by Oliver Sudden

Desert Crossing
   by I. Rhoda Camel

Candle-Vaulting
   by Jack B. Nimble

Happy New Year!
   by Mary Christmas

You're Kidding!
    by Shirley U. Joked

Webster's Words
    by Dick Shunnary

Those Funny People
    by Joe Kur

Winning the Race
    by Vic Tree

Crocodile Jealousy
    by Ali Gator

Fun Games
    by R. Kade

I Need Insurance
    by Justin Case

Whatchamacallit
    by Thingum E. Bob

I'm Someone Else
    by Ima Nonna Muss

It's Contagious!
    by Lucas Measles

The Great Escape
    by Freida Convict

Breaking the Law
    by Kermit A. Krime

Cooking Spaghetti
   by Al Dente

Proper Housekeeping
   by Lotta Dust

Mountain Climbing
   by Andover Hand

Poetry in Baseball
   by Homer Un

I Love Mathematics
   by Adam Up

Exercise on Wheels
   by Cy Kling

Stringed Instruments
by Viola Player

Open Air
by Alf Resco

Smash His Lobster
by Buster Crabbe

In the Arctic Ocean
by Isa Berg

Modern Tree Watches
by Anna Log

Forbidden
by Nada Loud

Snakes of the World
   by Anna Conda

The Housing Problem
   by Rufus Leeking

Artificial Clothing
   by Polly Ester

More for Your Money
   by Max Amize

Two Thousand Pounds
   by Juan Ton

Overweight Vegetables
   by O. Beets

Mineralogy for Giants
   by Chris Tall

Bring to the Store
   by Shaw Ping List

Almost Missed the Bus
   by Justin Time

My Life in the Gutter
   by Yves Trough

Things to Cook Soup In
   by Stu Potts

Tyrant of the Potatoes
   by Dick Tater

I Hate Monday Mornings

by Gaetan Oop

The Fall of a Watermelon

by S. Platt

Military Defeats

by Major Disaster and
General Mayhem

Judging Fast Food

by Warren Berger

I Lost My Balance

by Eileen Dover and
Paul Down

Kangaroo Illnesses
    by Marcus Wallaby, M.D.

Irish Plants
    by Phil O'Dendron

Musicals
    by The Okay Chorale

A Whole Lot of Cats
    by Kitt N. Caboodle

Working with Diamonds
    by Jules Sparkle

Laws of Suffering
    by Grin and Barrett

Errors and Accidents
  by Miss Takes and Miss Haps

Where to Find Islands
  by Archie Pelago

French Overpopulation
  by Francis Crowded

I Like Weeding Gardens
  by Manuel Labor

Who Stole a Cookie?
  by Howard I. Know

Are We There Yet?
  by Miles Away

The Excitement of Trees
by I. M. Board

A Bundle of Laughs
by Vera Funny

Artificial Weight
by Andy Gravity

Fifty Yards to the Outhouse
by Willy Makit

Foot Problems of Lumberjacks
by Paul Bunion

Where are the Animals?
by Darryn de Barn

Walking to School
   by Misty Bus

The Number Game
   by Cal Q. Later

Deep in Debt
   by Owen A. Lot

Robotics
   by Cy Borg

Bungee Jumping
   by Hugo First

Taking Tests
   by B. A. Wiseman

Computer Memory
   by Meg A. Byte

The Membership List
   by Ross Terr

All About Flowers
   by Chris Anthymum

The Lost Scout
   by Werram Eye

How to Eat Cereal
   by Peor A. Bowl

Green Vegetables
   by Q. Cumber

Neat Shirts
> by Preston Ironed

Unclean!
> by Phil Thee

How to Overcome Stress
> by R. E. Lax

I'm Exhausted
> by Rhonda Marathon

How to Succeed in School
> by Rita Lott

Uncooked Soup
> by Rob Roth

How to Apply Makeup
> by Rosie Cheeks

The Squeaking Cupboard
> by Rusty Hinge

Imitating Mozart
> by Sam Fony

All Alone
> by Saul E. Terry

Let's See That Again
> by Schlomo Replay

Circle Perimeter
> by Sir Cumference

Deceleration
> by Sloane Down

Don't Sit
> by Stan Dupp

Some Like It Sweet
> by Sugar Kane

Bad Cow Jokes
> by Terry Bull

Best Takeaways
> by Terry Yaki

Keep them in Suspense
> by Toby Continued

Bad Beverages
  by Travis Tea

Untied Sneakers
  by Tyrone Shoelaces

Why Won't the Car Move?
  by Vlad Tires

Woman in Danger
  by Warner Quick

Bad Gardening
  by Wilt Ed Plant

It Wasn't Her
  by Zoe Didit

The Arctic Oceans
by I. C. Waters

Together for a Year
by Annie Versary

The Old Tapes
by Cass Ette

Throw It Away
by D. Sposable

Favorite Pizza Toppings
by Pepe Roni

Third of Five
by Quinn Tuplet

Find Another Lonely Heart
by Q. Pid

House Construction
by Bill Jerome Holme

BIBLE BELLY LAUGHS

Who was the greatest female businessperson in the Bible?

> *Pharaoh's daughter. She went down to the bank of the Nile and drew out a little prophet.*

Who is the shortest person in the Bible?

> *Bildad the Shuhite (shoe-height). Nehemiah (knee-high-miah) was a close second.*

When was meat first mentioned in the Bible?

> *When Noah took Ham into the ark.*

How long did Cain dislike his brother?

As long as he was Abel.

At what time of day was Adam created?

A little before Eve.

Where is the first math homework problem in the Bible?

When God told Adam and Eve to go forth and multiply.

Why did Noah have to discipline the chickens on the Ark?

Because they were using fowl language.

Where is medicine first mentioned in the Bible?

When God gave Moses two tablets.

What's the best way to study the Bible?

You Luke into it.

What kind of man was Boaz before he married Ruth?

He was Ruthless.

Who was the greatest comedian in the Bible?

Samson. He brought the house down.

Which servant of God was the biggest lawbreaker in the Bible?

Moses. He broke all ten commandments at once.

Which area of Palestine was especially wealthy?

The area around Jordan. The banks were always overflowing.

Which Bible character had no
earthly parents besides Adam and Eve?

Joshua, son of Nun.

Why didn't they play cards on the Ark?

Because Noah was standing on the deck.

Why couldn't Jonah trust the ocean?

Because he knew there was something fishy about it.

Did Adam ever have a date with Eve?

No, just an apple.

Where was Solomon's temple located?

On the side of his head.

Where is the first tennis match mentioned in the Bible?

When Moses served on Pharaoh's court.

What did Adam say on the day before Christmas?

It's Christmas, Eve!

How does the Apostle Paul make his coffee?

Hebrews it.

Why didn't Noah go fishing on the Ark?

Because he only had two worms.

How do we know Peter was wealthy?

By his net income.

Who was the smartest man in the Bible?

Abraham. He knew a Lot.

Who was the fastest runner in the race?

Adam was the first in the human race.

What animal couldn't Noah trust?

The cheetah.

On the Ark, Noah probably got milk from the cow. What did he get from the ducks?

Quackers.

Where is the first baseball game in the Bible?

In the big inning. Eve stole first and Adam stole second.

Why didn't Cain bring God an acceptable offering?

Because he wasn't Abel!

Why couldn't they have apples on Noah's Ark?

Because everything was in pears.

How many people went on the Ark before Noah?

Three. The Bible says, "Noah went forth."

Why did the bees take so long to get out of the Ark when the doors finally opened?

They were in the archives (ark-hives).

What kind of lights did Noah use during night?

Floodlights.

AROUND THE HOUSE

What kind of coat can only
be put on wet?

A coat of paint.

What time is it when an elephant sits
on your fence?

Time to get a new fence.

What turns into another story?

A spiral staircase.

What constantly eats,
but is always hungry?

A fire.

What goes up and down the stairs
without moving?

Carpet.

What type of dress can't you wear?

An address.

What always goes to bed
with its shoes on?

A horse.

Why are teddy bears never hungry?

They're always stuffed.

What type of house weighs the least?

A lighthouse.

Why can't a bicycle
stand up on its own?

Because it is two tired.

How do you have a party in space?

You Planet.

How do you make antifreeze?

You steal her blanket.

What did the steak say to the beef?

So, we meat again.

Who gets rid of eggs?

The eggs-terminator.

What jumps from cake to cake and smells of almonds?

Tarzipan.

Have you ever tried to eat a clock?

It's very time consuming.

What tastes better than it smells?

Your tongue.

ABSURD ANIMALS

What side of a cat has the most fur?

The outside.

How do dog catchers get paid?

By the pound.

What's another type of key that can't open a door?

A donkey.

Where do fish keep their money?

A riverbank.

What kind of fish chases a mouse?

A catfish.

What do they call pastors in Germany?

German Shepherds.

What animal needs to wear a wig?

A bald eagle.

What do you get if you cross a snake and a lego set?

A boa constructor.

Why do giraffes take so long to apologize?

It takes them a long time to swallow their pride.

How do snails talk to each other?

By using shell phones.

Why did the man buy a donkey?

*He thought he might
get a kick out of it.*

**What do you get when you cross
a snowman with a vampire bat?**

Frostbite.

**Why did the kid throw the butter
out the window?**

To see the butter fly.

**Why did the canary sit on the ladder
to sing?**

It wanted to reach the high notes.

Where do mice park their boats?

At the hickory dickory dock.

Where do orcas hear music?

At the orca-stra.

What do you do if a dog chews up your dictionary?

Take the words out of his mouth.

Why do cows wear bells?

Because their horns don't work.

What do you call an alligator who steals?

A crookodile.

Why did the lamb cross the road?

To get to the baaaarber shop.

What has four legs and says,
"Oom, oom?"

A cow walking backwards.

What do you get when you plant a frog?

A croak tree.

How is a dog like a phone?

It has collar ID.

What would happen if pigs could fly?

The price of bacon would go up.

What do whales eat?

Fish and ships.

What do sardines call a submarine?

A can of people.

What do fish take to stay healthy?

Vitamin sea.

What's a shark's favorite sandwich?

Peanut butter and jellyfish.

Why don't bears wear shoes?

What's the point? They'd still have bear feet!

What kind of cars do cats drive?

Catillacs.

What do camels use to hide themselves?

Camelflauge.

What do you call an untidy hippo?

A hippopotamess.

What do you call a cow that twitches?

Beef jerky.

What's a lion's favorite state?

Maine.

What do cats like for breakfast?

Mice Krispies.

What is a horse's favorite sport?

Stable tennis.

What game do elephants play
when riding in the car?

Squash.

Where do horses live?

In the neigh-borhood.

What happened when 500 hares got loose downtown?

Police had to comb the area.

Where do sharks come from?

Finland.

How many skunks does it take to make a big stink?

A phew.

SRSLY. BEST. JOKES. EVER.

JOKES FOR KIDS

CHANTELLE GRACE

COLOR COMEDY

What happens when you throw a white hat into the Black Sea?

It gets wet.

What's black and white, black and white, and black and white?

A zebra caught in a revolving door.

What's black and white, black and white, and green?

Two skunks fighting over a pickle.

When is a black dog not a black dog?

When it's a grey-hound.

Why did the tomato turn red?

Because it saw the salad dressing.

What's orange and sounds like a parrot?

A carrot.

What bird is always sad?

The blue jay.

What's green and smells like blue paint?

Green paint.

What color is a burp?

Burple.

What do you do when you find
a blue elephant?

Cheer it up.

What do you do with a green monster?

Wait until it's ripe.

What happened when a red ship crashed
into a blue ship?

The crew was marooned.

What would you call the USA if everyone
had a pink car?

A pink carnation.

What is a cheerleader's favorite color?

Yeller.

GEOGRAPHY GUFFAWS

What goes through towns, up and over hills, but doesn't move?

The road.

What did the little mountain say to the big mountain?

"Hi Cliff."

What do you call a funny mountain?

Hill-arious.

What is the best day to go
to the beach?

Sunday, of course.

What stays on the ground
but never gets dirty?

A shadow.

Name a city where no one goes?

Electricity.

What stays in the corner and travels
all over the world?

A stamp.

What is the tallest building
in the world?

*The library because it has
the most stories.*

What did the stamp say
to the envelope?

"Stick with me and we will go places."

What did the ground say
to the earthquake?

"You crack me up."

Why does the Mississippi river
see so well?

Because it has 4 i's.

MONEY MADNESS

Where does a penguin keep its money?

In a snow bank.

How do dinosaurs pay their bills?

With Tyrannosaurus checks.

Where can you always find money?

In the dictionary.

Why did the robber take a bath
before he stole from the bank?

He wanted to make a clean getaway.

What did one penny say
to the other penny?

"Together we make cents."

What is brown and has a head
and a tail but no legs?

A penny.

What did the duck say after
he went shopping?

"Put it on my bill."

What has a hundred heads
and a hundred tails?

One hundred pennies.

Why can't you borrow money
from a leprechaun?

Because they're always a little short.

Why didn't the quarter roll down the hill with the nickel?

Because it had more cents.

What English word has three consecutive double letters?

Bookkeeper.

Where does success come before work?

In the dictionary.

Why did the businessman put a clock under his desk?

Because he wanted to work over-time.

SCHOOL SILLIES

Why did the nose not want to go to school?

It was tired of getting picked on.

How do you get straight A's?

By using a ruler.

What did the pen say to the pencil?

"So, what's your point?"

Why did the kid study in the airplane?

*Because he wanted
a higher education.*

How did the music teacher get locked
out of the classroom?

His keys were inside the piano.

What do elves learn in school?

The elf-abet.

What did you learn in school today?

*Not enough,
I have to go back tomorrow.*

What object is king of the classroom?

The ruler.

What did the pencil sharpener say to the pencil?

"Stop going in circles and get to the point."

What do librarians take with them when they go fishing?

Bookworms.

What vegetables do librarians like?

Peas.

Why did the clock in the cafeteria run slow?

It always went back four seconds.

Why didn't the sun go to college?

Because it already had a million degrees.

Where do the pianists go for vacation?

The Florida Keys.

What is the smartest state?

Alabama—it has four A's and one B.

What did the paper say to the pencil?

"Write on."

What kind of meals do math teachers eat?

Square meals.

Teacher: Now class, whatever I ask, I want you to all answer at once. How much is six plus four?

Class: At once.

Why didn't the two 4's want
any dinner?

Because they already 8.

What is a math teacher's
favorite season?

Sum-mer.

What is a butterfly's favorite subject
at school?

Mothematics.

What do you get when you divide
the circumference of a Jack-o-lantern
by its diameter?

Pumpkin Pi.

What did zero say to the number eight?

"Nice belt."

Teacher: Why are you doing your multiplication on the floor?

Student: You told me not to use tables.

Why did the teacher wear sunglasses?

Because his class was so bright.

Teacher: Didn't I tell you to stand at the end of the line?

Student: I tried but there was someone already there.

How is an English teacher like a judge?

They both give out sentences.

Teacher: You missed school yesterday, didn't you?

Student: Not really.

Why did the teacher go to the beach?

To test the water.

Teacher: If I had six oranges in one hand and seven apples in the other, what would I have?

Student: Big hands.

Teacher: If you got $20 from five people, what would you have?

Student: A new bike.

Teacher: I hope I didn't see you looking at John's exam.

Student: I hope you didn't either.

Teacher: What is the shortest month?

Student: May—it only has three letters.

Why did the teacher turn the lights on?

Because his class was so dim.

What do you do if a teacher rolls her eyes at you?

Pick them up and roll them back.

Why did the teacher write on the window?

Because he wanted the lesson to be very clear.

Why was everyone so tired on April 1st?

They had just finished a March of 31 days.

Which hand is it better to write with?

Neither, it's best to write with a pen.

Why does the calendar seem
so popular?

It has so many dates.

Why did the music teacher need
a ladder?

To reach the high notes.

What's the worst thing you're likely
to find in the school cafeteria?

The food.

Why aren't you doing well in history?

*Because the teacher keeps asking
about things that happened before
I was born.*

What has forty feet and sings?

The school choir.

What makes music on your head?

A head band.

In which school do you learn
to make ice cream?

Sundae school.

CLOTHING CHEER

What do you call a belt
with a watch on it?

A waist of time.

What did the tie say to the hat?

*"You go on ahead
and I'll hang around."*

Why did the woman go outdoors
with her purse open?

*Because she expected some change
in the weather.*

Why don't you wear a cardboard belt?

That would be a waist of paper.

Why did the clown wear loud socks?

So his feet wouldn't fall asleep.

Why did the leopard wear
a striped shirt?

So it wouldn't be spotted.

What's the biggest problem
with snow boots?

They melt.

What do you call doing 2,000 pounds
of laundry?

Washing-ton.

What kind of shoes do all spies wear?

Sneakers.

Does your shirt have holes in it?

No.

Then how did you put it on?

SPORTS SLAPSTICK

Why can't Cinderella play soccer?

Because she's always running away from the ball.

Why do basketball players love donuts?

Because they dunk them.

What's a golfer's favorite letter?

T.

What is an insect's favorite sport?

Cricket.

What do you call a pig
who plays basketball?

A ball hog.

How is a baseball team similar
to a pancake?

They both need a good batter.

What animal is best at hitting
a baseball?

A bat.

At what sport do waiters do really well?

Tennis, because they can serve.

How do basketball players stay cool
during the game?

They stand close to the fans.

What do hockey players and magicians have in common?

Both do hat tricks.

Why did the man keep doing the backstroke?

Because he just ate and didn't want to swim on a full stomach.

What is the hardest part about skydiving?

The ground.

KNOCK-KNOCK
KNEE-SLAPPERS

Knock, knock.

Who's there?

Little old lady.

Little old lady who?

Wow! I didn't know you could yodel.

Knock, knock.

Who's there?

Cowsgo.

Cowsgo who?

No they don't; cowsgo moo.

Knock, knock.

Who's there?

Interrupting cow.

Interrupting cow wh...

Moo!

Knock, knock.

Who's there?

Doris.

Doris who?

Doris locked; that's why I knocked.

Knock, knock.

Who's there?

Cash.

Cash who?

I knew you were a nut.

Knock, knock.

Who's there?

Ash.

Ash who?

Bless you.

Knock, knock.

Who's there?

Nobel.

Nobel who?

No bell, that's why I knocked.

Knock, knock.

Who's there?

Leaf.

Leaf who?

Leaf me alone.

Knock, knock.

Who's there?

Aaron.

Aaron who?

Why Aaron you opening the door?

Knock, knock.

Who's there?

Tank.

Tank who?

You're welcome.

Knock, knock.

Who's there?

Hawaii.

Hawaii who?

I'm fine; Hawaii you?

Knock, knock.

Who's there?

Who.

Who who?

Is there an owl in there?

Knock, knock.

Who's there?

Anita.

Anita who?

Anita borrow a pencil.

Knock, knock.

Who's there?

Figs.

Figs who?

Figs the doorbell; it's broken.

Knock, knock.

Who's there?

Alice.

Alice who?

Alice fair in love and war.

Knock, knock.

Who's there?

Annie.

Annie who?

*Annie thing you can do
I can do better.*

Knock, knock.

Who's there?

Yukon.

Yukon who?

Yukon say that again.

Knock, knock.

Who's there?

Boo.

Boo who?

Well you don't have to cry about it.

Knock, knock.

Who's there?

Theodore.

Theodore who?

Theodore is stuck and it won't open.

Knock, knock.

Who's there?

Cher.

Cher who?

Cher would be nice if you opened the door.

Knock, knock

Who's there?

Amos.

Amos who?

A mosquito bit me.

Knock, knock.

Who's there?

Police.

Police who?

Police let us in; it's cold out here.

Knock, knock.

Who's there?

Amarillo.

Amarillo who?

Amarillo nice guy.

Knock, knock.

Who's there?

Irish.

Irish who?

Irish you a happy St. Patrick's Day.

Knock, knock.

Who's there?

Kook.

Kook who?

Don't call me cuckoo!

NATURE NONSENSE

How can you tell that a tree is a dogwood tree?

By its bark.

What kind of hair do oceans have?

Wavy.

What kind of flower grows on your face?

Tulips.

What did the little tree say
to the big tree?

"Leaf me alone."

Why did the girl bring a book
and a pen to the garden?

She wanted to weed and write.

Did you hear the one about
the oak tree?

It's a-corny one.

Where does seaweed go to look
for a job?

The kelp wanted section.

What did the big flower say
to the little flower?

"Hey, bud."

Why did the pine tree get into trouble?

Because it was being knotty.

How can you tell the ocean is friendly?

It waves.

What did the tree do when
the bank closed?

It started a new branch.

Who cleans the bottom of the ocean?

A mer-maid.

What washes up on very small beaches?

Microwaves.

What flower doesn't tell the truth?

A li-lac.

What did the gardener say when she dropped her flowers?

"Whoopsie daises."

FARM FUNNIES

What's a cow's favorite game?

Moosical chairs.

What do you call a pig with no legs?

A groundhog.

How do pigs write top secret messages?

With invisible oink.

How did the farmer mend his pants?

With cabbage patches.

What do you call a sheep with no head and no legs?

A cloud.

Where do cows go for entertainment?

To the moo-vies.

Why did the farmer ride his horse to town?

It was too heavy to carry.

Where do sheep go on vacation?

To the baaaaaahamas.

What do you call a happy cowboy?

A jolly rancher.

What is a pig's favorite color?

Mahogany.

How do you fit more pigs on your farm?

Build a sty-scraper.

When does a horse talk?

Whinny wants to.

What did the farmer call the cow
that had no milk?

An udder failure.

What do you call a sheep covered
in chocolate?

A candy baa.

What do you call an emotional cow?

Moo-dy.

What do you get when you play Tug-of-War with a pig?

Pulled pork.

What does a mixed-up hen lay?

Scrambled eggs.

Why did the pig cross the road?

He got boared.

What sickness do horses hate the most?

Hay fever!

How do you take a sick pig
to the hospital?

In a hambulance.

What's the most musical part
of a chicken?

The drumstick.

What do you call a pig
that drives recklessly?

A road hog.

What is a sheep's favorite game?

Baa-dminton.

Where do you find a chicken
with no legs?

Exactly where you left it.

What's the difference between
a horse and the weather?

> *One is reined up and the other
> rains down.*

What do you get when you cross
a cow and a duck?

> *Milk and quackers.*

Where do bulls get their messages?

> *On a bull-etin board.*

What do you call a cow that won't
give milk?

> *A milk dud.*

Who is the smartest pig in the world?

> *Ein-swine.*

What do you call it when it rains
chickens and ducks?

Foul weather.

What did the bad sheep want to do?

Wool the world.

Have you heard about
the cow astronaut?

He landed on the moooon.

Where do sheep go
to get their haircut?

The baabaa shop.

Why did the cow cross the road?

To get to the udder side.

Why do cows wear bells?

Their horns don't work.

What do you get when you cross a cow and a goat?

A coat.

What do you call a cow that plays a musical instrument?

A moo-sician.

What does it mean if you find a horseshoe in the road?

Some poor horse is walking around in its socks.

What do you call a sleeping bull?

A bull dozer.

Why did the turkey cross the road?

It was the chicken's day off.

Which side of a chicken
has the most feathers?

The outside.

Why do hens lay eggs?

If they dropped them, they'd break.

What do you get if you cross a chicken
with a cow?

Roost beef.

What do you call a horse that lives
next door?

A neigh-bor.

Why did the cow jump over the moon?

Because the farmer had cold hands!

What kind of car does a farmer drive?

A cornvertable.

SPACE
SIDE-SPLITTERS

Why didn't people like the restaurant on the moon?

Because there was no atmosphere.

What do astronauts cook on?

Flying saucers.

Why did the baby go to outer space?

To visit the milky way.

What does an astronaut use to keep his feet warm?

A space heater.

How do you know when the moon is going broke?

When it's down to its last quarter.

How does the barber cut the moon's hair?

E-clipse it.

What holds the sun up in the sky?

Sunbeams.

What is the center of gravity?

The letter V.

What do you call a peanut
in a spacesuit?

An astronut.

What did the alien say to the garden?

Take me to your weeder.

What kind of plates do they use
on Venus?

Flying saucers.

What does an astronaut eat
for dinner?

Nothing, he went out for launch.

TRANSPORTATION TICKLES

When does a cart come before a horse?

In the dictionary.

Why don't traffic lights ever go swimming?

Because they take too long to change.

What vehicle did the crazy man drive?

A loco-motive.

Why did the man put his car
in the oven?

He wanted a hot rod.

What is a motorcycle called
when it laughs?

A Yamahahaha.

What does a houseboat turn into
when it grows up?

A township.

What only starts to work after
it's fired?

A rocket.

What's the worst vegetable to serve
on a boat?

Leeks.

How do trains hear?

Through their engine-ears.

What did one elevator say to the other elevator?

"I think I'm coming down with something."

What do you call a flying police officer?

A helicopper.

What kind of car did the Pilgrims drive?

A Plymouth.

RIDDLE RIOTS

If you were in a race and passed the person in second place, what place would you be in?

Second place.

What word looks the same backwards and upside down?

Swims.

What gets bigger and bigger as you take more away from it?

A hole.

How many months have 28 days?

All of them.

What has two hands, a round face, always runs, but stays in place?

A clock.

What breaks when you say it?

Silence.

Can you spell rotten with two letters?

DK.

How can you spell cold with two letters?

IC.

What starts with a P, ends with an E, and has a hundred letters in it?

Post Office.

What can run but can't walk?

The water faucet.

What is taken before you get it?

Your picture.

A rooster laid an egg on a barn roof. Which way would it roll?

Roosters don't lay eggs, hens do.

Chickens rise when the rooster crows, but when do ducks get up?

At the quack of dawn.

Why can't your nose be 12 inches long?

Because then it would be a foot.

Why did the lazy man want a job in a bakery?

So he could loaf around.

What goes up, but never comes down?

Your age.

What is full of holes but can still hold water?

A sponge.

What's as big as a dinosaur but weighs nothing?

Its shadow.

What cheese is made backwards?

Edam.

What geometric figure is like
a lost parrot?

A polygon.

Why do dogs run in circles?

*Because it's too hard to run
in squares.*

How do you confuse a fish?

*Put it in a round fishbowl
and tell it to go to the corner.*

What do you call a line of rabbits
walking backwards?

A receding hareline.

What does a thesaurus eat
for breakfast?

A synonym roll.

What do you get when you cross an owl
and an oyster?

Pearls of wisdom.

What do you call fifty penguins
at the North Pole?

*Really lost, because penguins live
in the Southern Hemisphere.*

What's worse than a worm
in your apple?

Half a worm in your apple.

Why are A's like flowers?

Because bees come after them.

What do you call a fly without wings?

A walk.

What letter can hurt you if you get too close?

B.

HOLIDAY HILARITY

Why did pilgrims' pants always fall down?

Because they wore their belt buckle on their hat.

Why does Santa Claus like to go down the chimney?

Because it soots him!

What happened when the Thanksgiving turkey got into a fight?

He got the stuffing knocked out of him.

What do Santa's elves do after school?

Their gnomework!

Why do students do so poorly after Thanksgiving?

Because everything gets marked down after the holidays.

Why didn't the skeleton go to the dance?

Because he had no-body to go with.

What always comes at the end of Thanksgiving?

The G.

What do snowmen like to eat for breakfast?

Frosted Flakes.

Who isn't hungry on Thanksgiving?

The turkey, because he's already stuffed.

Why don't skeletons fight?

They don't have the guts.

What happens when a snowman throws a temper tantrum?

He has a meltdown.

DINOSAUR DISCUSSION

What do you call a dinosaur that smashes everything in its path?

Tyrannosaurus wrecks.

Why did the dinosaur paint her toenails red?

So she could hide in the strawberry patch.

What do you call a tyrannosaurus that talks and talks and talks?

A dino-bore.

What should you do if you find
a dinosaur in your bed?

Find somewhere else to sleep.

What do you get when a dinosaur walks
through the strawberry patch?

Strawberry jam.

How did the dinosaur feel after
he ate a pillow?

Down in the mouth.

What do you get when a dinosaur
sneezes?

Out of the way.

What do you get if you cross
a Triceratops with a kangaroo?

A Tricera-hops.

What do you get if you cross a pig
with a dinosaur?

Jurassic Pork.

Which dinosaurs were
the best policemen?

Tricera-cops.

Where do prehistoric reptiles like
to go on vacation?

To the dino-shore.

How do dinosaurs pay their bills?

With Tyrannosaurus checks.

Why did the Apatosaurus devour
the factory?

Because she was a plant eater.

How can you tell if there's a dinosaur in the refrigerator?

The door won't close.

How do you make a dinosaur float?

Put a scoop of ice cream in a glass of root beer and add a dinosaur.

FOOD FRENZY

How do you make a milk shake?

Give it a good scare.

How do you make a walnut laugh?

Crack it up.

Why did the girl sprinkle sugar on her pillow before she went to sleep?

So she would have sweet dreams.

What kind of keys do kids like to carry?

Cookies!

Why don't they serve chocolate in prison?

Because it makes you break out.

What is a scarecrow's favorite fruit?

Straw-berries.

What does a nosey pepper do?

It gets jalapeno business.

What do you call a fake noodle?

An impasta.

What do you call cheese that doesn't belong to you?

Nacho cheese!

Why did the boy go out with a prune?

Because he couldn't find a date.

Have you heard the joke about
the butter?

I better not tell you; it might spread.

What runs but doesn't get anywhere?

A refrigerator.

What kind of crackers do firemen
like the most?

Firecrackers.

Why was the cookie sad?

*Because its mom was a wafer
too long.*

Why did the boy stare at the label
on the orange juice all day?

Because the carton said concentrate.

CRAZY CREATURES

How do rabbits stay in shape?

They do a lot of hare-obics.

What do you call a pile of kittens?

A meowntain.

What kind of bird can carry
the most weight?

The crane.

What animal gets in trouble at school?

The cheetah.

Is it raining cats and dogs?

It's okay, as long as it doesn't rein-deer.

What bird is with you at every meal?

A swallow.

How do you catch a squirrel?

Climb up a tree and act like a nut.

What do you give a sick bird?

Tweetment.

What is a frog's favorite cold drink?

Croak-a-cola.

What do you call a rabbit comedian?

A funny bunny.

Did you hear the story about
the peacock?

> Yes, it's a beautiful tale.

What do you call a lizard who is elected
to Congress?

> Rep. Tile.

Why can't a leopard hide?

> It will always be spotted.

What is it called when a cat wins
a dog show?

> A cat-has-trophy.

Why don't you see penguins
in the United Kingdom?

> Because they're afraid of Wales.

What do you get if you cross a chili pepper, a shovel, and a terrier?

A hot-diggity-dog.

What does a duck like to eat with soup?

Quackers.

What did the dog say when he sat on sandpaper?

"Ruff."

How can you tell which are the oldest rabbits?

Just look for the gray hares.

Who did Bambi invite to his birthday party?

His nearest and deer-est friends.

Why do hummingbirds hum?

Because they forgot the words.

What do frogs wear on their feet?

Open toad shoes.

What do you get when you cross
a walrus with a bee?

A wallaby.

Why don't oysters share their pearls?

Because they're shellfish.

Why do birds fly south for the winter?

Because it's too far to walk.

How does a penguin build its house?

Igloos it together.

Where do fish sleep?

On a seabed.

What's noisier than a whooping crane?

A trumpeting swan.

What do you call a bird in the winter?

Brrr-d.

What do dogs eat at the movies?

Pup-corn.

How do mice feel when they are sick?

Mouserable.

What is the strongest creature
in the sea?

A mussel.

What do you get if you cross a canary and a 50-foot long snake?

A sing-a-long.

What kind of book does a rabbit like to read?

One with a hoppy ending.

What happens when a duck flies upside down?

It quacks up.

What do you get when you cross a parrot and a shark?

A bird that talks your ear off.

What do you call a duck who leads an orchestra?

A con-duck-tor.

What do you get when you cross a frog and a popsicle?

A hopsicle.

Where do fish go when their things go missing?

The Lost-and-Flounder Department.

How do penguins drink?

Out of beak-ers.

What did the Dalmatian say after eating dinner?

"That hit the spot."

What did the duck wear to his wedding?

A Duxedo.

What is a dog's favorite dessert?

Pup-cakes.

What do you get if you cross a dog
and an airplane?

A jet setter.

What do you call a frog
with no hind legs?

Unhoppy.

Which animal grows down?

A duck.

How do oysters call their friends?

On shell phones.

Why didn't the butterfly go
to the dance?

Because it was a moth ball.

What do you call a wet baby owl?

A moist-owlette.

What's the difference between a guitar
and a fish?

You can't tuna fish.

Where do chimps get their information?

From the ape vine.

What do you call a bear caught
in the rain?

A drizzly bear.

When did the fly fly?

When the spider spied her.

What did the buffalo say to his son when he left for college?

Bison.

Why did the cowboy buy a daschund?

Someone told him to get along little doggy.

What do penguins wear on their heads?

Ice caps.

What do you get when you cross a frog and a bunny?

A ribbit.

Why did the owl invite his friends over?

He didn't want to be owl by himself.

What did one frog say to the other?

"Time is fun when you're having flies."

What is a frog's favorite music?

Hip hop.

What do you get when you cross
a penguin and an alligator?

*I don't know, but don't try to fix
its bow tie.*

What do you call two ants that run
away to get married?

Ant-elopes.

How do fleas travel from place to place?

They itch-hike.

What do you get if you cross a centipede and a parrot?

A walkie-talkie.

What are caterpillars afraid of?

Dogger-pillars.

What is an insect's favorite sport?

Cricket.

What kind of fly has a frog in its throat?

A hoarse fly.

WRITE YOUR
FAVORITE JOKE HERE

WRITE YOUR
FAVORITE JOKE HERE

WRITE YOUR
FAVORITE JOKE HERE